Bargello Plus

Also by Mira Silverstein

FUN WITH BARGELLO

FUN WITH APPLIQUE

BARGELLO PLUS

By Mira Silverstein

PHOTOGRAPHS BY SALVATORE D. LOPES

DIAGRAMS BY ROBERTA FRAUWIRTH

—

Charles Scribner's Sons, New York

Acknowledgments

I wish to thank my husband and our children for their encouragement and invaluable help during the long months when this book was being prepared.

Many thanks to the wonderful people who worked with me in a professional capacity and helped enhance this book with their individual talents: Sal and Shari Lopes, Roberta Frauwirth, Elise Silverstein, and book designer Ron Farber; to Mr. Girard Goodenow of Suzy Girard Inc. and Mrs. Denise Welch of denà designs inc. for their special assistance and permission to use some of their painted canvases, and to my friends Denise Strauss, Gigi Strauss, and Debbie Mayer, for helping me finish the samples.

As always, a very special thank you to a very special lady, my editor, Elinor Parker.

I dedicate this book to my husband

IRWIN M. SILVERSTEIN

Contents

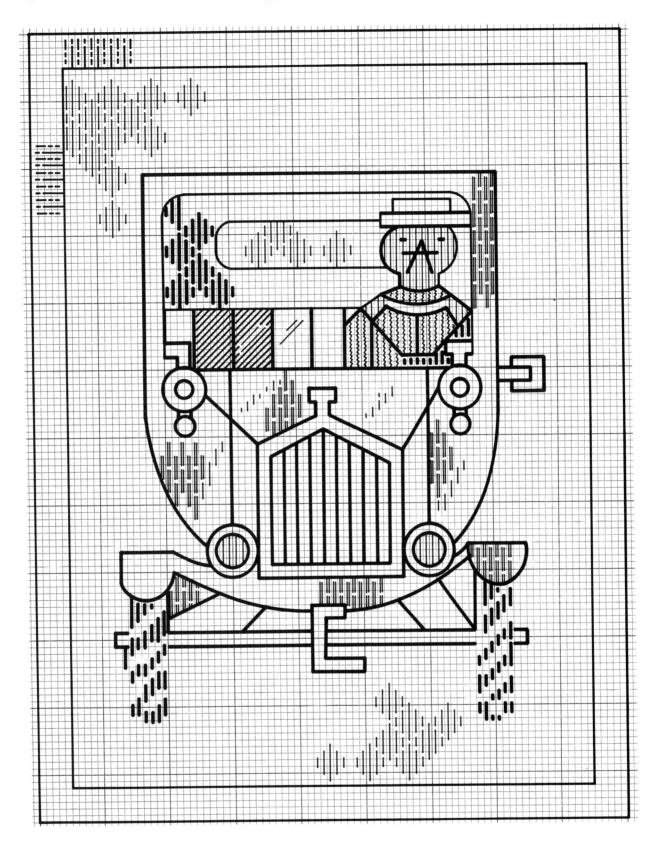

A charming design with multi-bargello stitches. The car
is worked in red yarn. "Silly Car" designed and worked
by denà designs, inc.

Introduction

Bargello embroidery is a form of needlepoint based on an upright stitch. It may be worked on any even-weave fabric such as linen, cotton, or wool, as well as the more popular needlepoint canvas.

Sometimes called Florentine embroidery, flame stitch, or Hungarian point, it was originally worked on softer fabrics, and is one of the oldest forms of needlework known.

The bargello stitch, if used well, is one of the most interesting and creative in the field of needlepoint. Once its properties are understood, it opens a world of possibilities. You will find that you are no longer limited to the simple linear or geometric designs.

Assuming that you know how to work bargello, this book is designed to assist you in working out an unlimited number of patterns. If you are not familiar with bargello embroidery, may I suggest that you read *Fun with Bargello* (Scribners). It was written especially for beginners and contains some valuable information on basic bargello stitches and linear design.

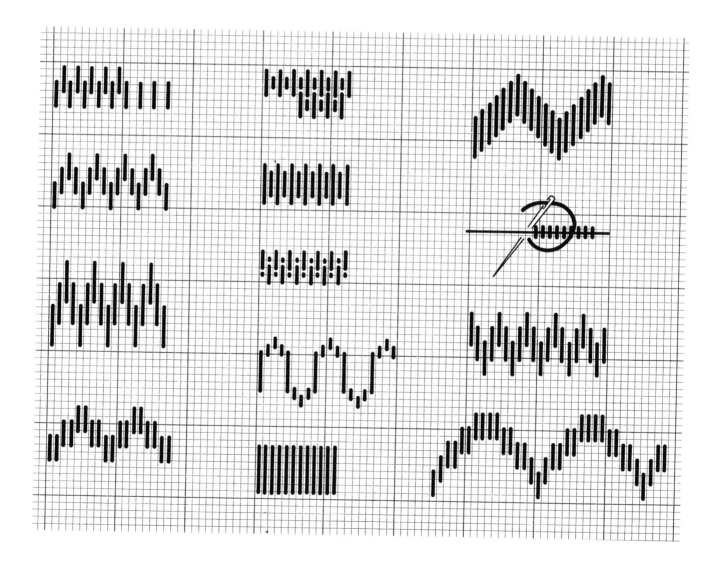

About the Stitch

O N pages 12-17 are various samples of bargello patterns. All the designs in this book are based on these patterns. The stitches may vary in length or an unusual color combination may make them appear different, but if you look closely, you will see that they are only the long and short upright bargello stitches.

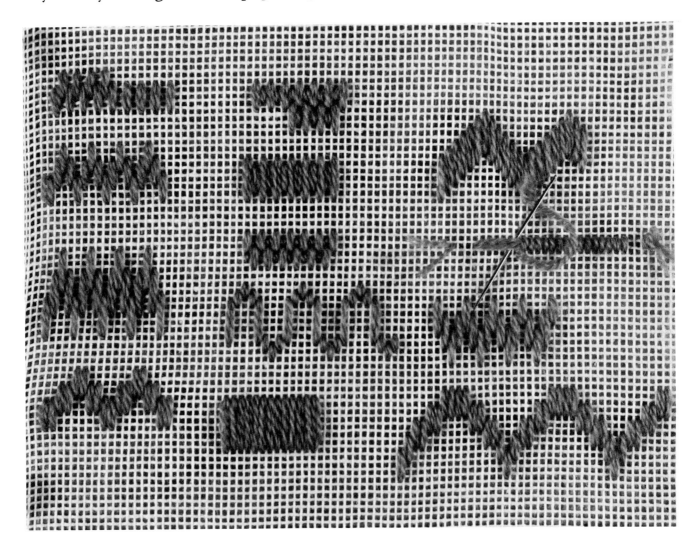

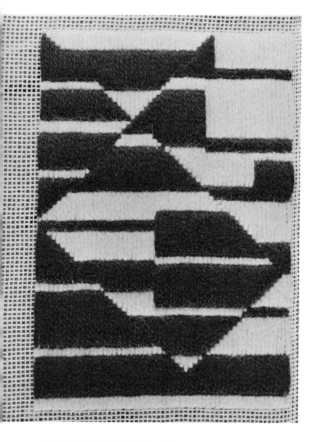

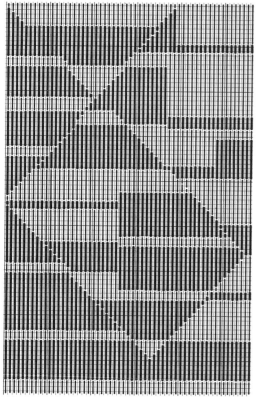

It is important to practice these stitches in order to get a better understanding of bargello and its properties. Work them softly over and under the strands of canvas. A simple brick stitch or a single-step design (see page 12) may be worked in one motion. That is, the needle goes in and out in one motion. The longer stitches and the very short ones will look better and straighter if worked in two motions. Needle goes in, thread is pulled through . . . needle comes out, thread is pulled through. Repeat.

After you try your hand at some of the stitches, see if you can change them. The length and number of stitches will change a design completely. For example on page 44 the two designs (19 and 20) are basically the same. However, one is worked with double stitches over four strands of canvas, whereas the other one is worked in single stitches over six strands of canvas.

Before establishing a design, explore its many possibilities. Elongate, shorten, widen, change color combinations. Frame it with a border. Don't settle for the ordinary. Try an original approach.

The long random stitches on page 48 (tiger) and page 34 (patchwork) are interesting and new. Canvas must be firm and the yarn must be kept from twisting by turning the needle toward you or counterclockwise, between thumb and forefinger after every stitch. Work slowly at first and don't pull the yarn too tight. Very long bargello stitches should be soft and full and cover the canvas completely without distorting it.

Whether a modern black and white design, pages 14, 15, a bold tiger skin, page 48, or the flowing look in patchwork pattern, page 34, the random width bargello is exciting. Needless to say, it is not recommended for pillows or accessories. It looks magnificent when framed.

If you like to work with stripes in random widths, you will find that a narrow stripe worked over one or two canvas strands is difficult to achieve unless it is worked in tramé. Simply knot a length of yarn and position the knot

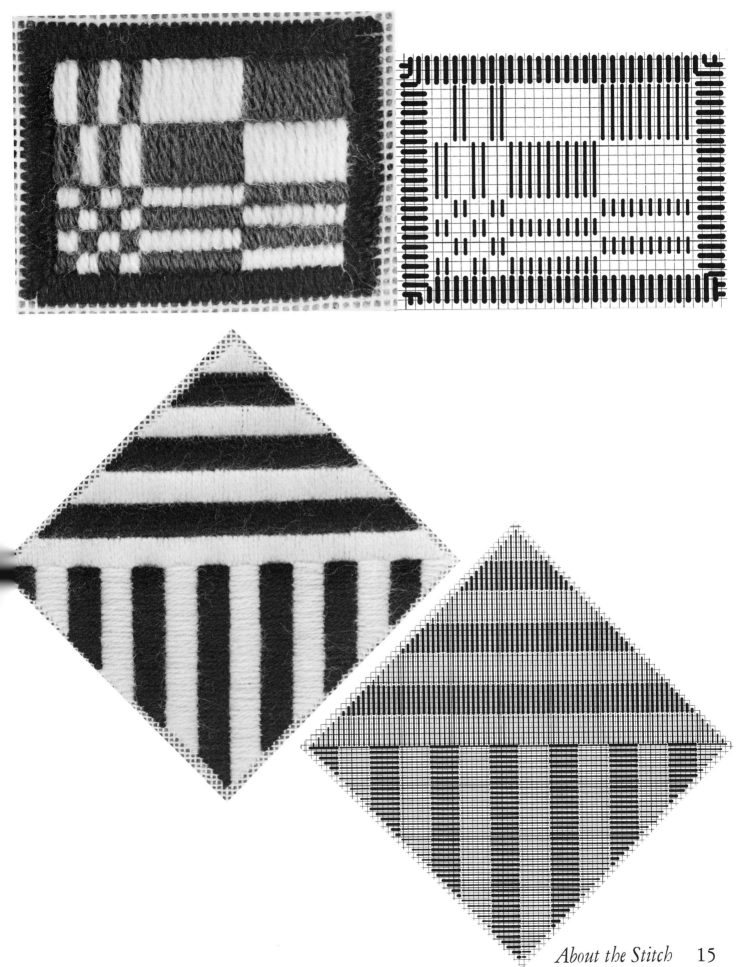

on the right side of your canvas, slightly outside your line of work. Carry the yarn across the face of the canvas in one straight line and tack it loosely on the other end. The length of yarn should be a little longer than the proposed stripe. With another strand of yarn of the same color work a line of bargello stitches over the tramé strand and one strand of canvas. Guide the tramé line with your left hand to keep the thread taut. For a slightly wider stripe, place tramé line between two parallel lines of canvas and work the bargello stitch over all of them. See page 12, color sample page 70.

Clip the knot and left-over tail end of yarn after stripe is finished. A little practice will do it.

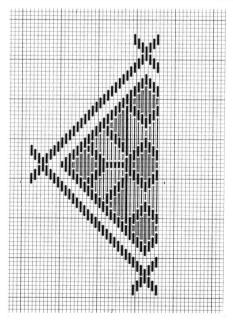
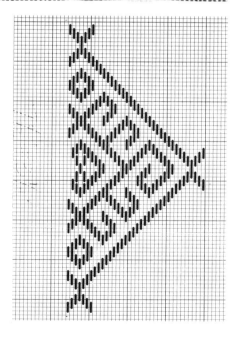

About Yarn

THE most commonly used needlepoint yarn in recent years has been the three-ply persian. Each strand is made up of three thinner strands that pull apart easily and may be used singly on very fine canvas. A full triple strand covers #12 canvas and if a little more fullness is needed, simply add another single strand. This affords one a high degree of flexibility when working with various types of canvas. A standard tapestry yarn, although of best quality, must fit the canvas perfectly. If it is too thin to be used in a single strand, chances are it is too heavy to be used doubled.

Three-ply persian type yarn is distributed through a number of dealers. Not all of them are of good quality. I suggest you try a small amount first. Most tapestry yarns are available in small skeins of about 8 to 10 yards each. Use up the entire skein. Work it with small stitches and large ones. Cut it in small lengths of about 24 inches. A good quality tapestry yarn should be able to withstand the friction of being pulled in and out of canvas for a length of 36 inches without losing its strength. If a 24-inch strand frays or breaks before it is finished, it is substandard and not worth buying and don't let anybody tell you otherwise. Such yarns are often priced the same as those of best quality, and, even if not, the difference is only a few pennies. When you work on a piece of needlepoint, the most important ingredient is the amount of time you invest in it. If it is worth your time, then it is worth the very best materials.

Standard tapestry yarns are excellent for bargello stitchery as long as they cover the canvas. Select yarns that are smooth and even-textured. Avoid using tightly twisted yarns or the textured novelties. Bargello is in itself a textured stitchery and should not be burdened with fancy yarns.

Tapestry yarns are available in skeins from one- to four-ounce sizes. The number of strands in each skein may vary because of the difference in thickness and length of strands. May I suggest that you check yarns available in your local shops and note the sizes of skeins available, number of strands in each skein, prices, and quality. You will find that if you are going to work out your own designs, you will get very little free information in most needlepoint supply stores. Learn to choose your own colors and estimate the amount of yarn you need. The simplest way is to work up a pattern or two with strands of yarn cut in a standard length. See how many strands you used and measure the size of the patterns. Project the number of patterns required in the overall area and you have the total number of strands needed. Add 10 per cent to be safe.

After a while, you will gain some experience and you will be able to estimate quite easily the amount of yarn and color selection for a given project. Other yarns suitable for bargello are six-strand embroidery cotton, smooth untwisted rayon, and silk. The cotton is very easy to use and looks lovely on small handbags and eyeglass cases on #16 canvas. It may be doubled on a #12 canvas but it does not always look as well. Cotton is color fast, washable, and has a mellow sheen. It may be used in borders on an even-weave embroidery linen on place mats, small tablecloths, or decorative trim on lightweight clothing. Bargello embroidery should not be washed in a washing machine. Hand washing and gentle care are recommended, so bear this in mind before deciding to work bargello on a dinner cloth for twelve.

Rayon and silk are a little trickier to use. They slip and slide and have a tendency to ravel and snarl. Work with lengths of not more than 12 inches and allow at least one inch at each end to weave under. I used rayons on the peacock design on page 33 doubled, on #12 canvas. I don't recommend it as a first project. You can achieve the same effect with six-strand embroidery cotton.

Note: If you double silk or rayon, use a 24-inch length and double it over the needle. Knot the ends together and weave in about one inch length on the underside before beginning. When your thread is finished, weave in the tail end (make sure it is at least one inch), cut, and clip the knot at the same time. Rayons and silks are available in small skeins at a nominal price. Buy a small amount and experiment.

Metallic yarns are also very attractive for special highlights. Work slowly with short strands.

Heavy rug yarns in wool and rayon are suitable for bargello stitchery. The heavier canvases such as #5 and #4 are available only in double mesh. To cover this heavy canvas, you might have to use two or even three strands of rug yarn. Use larger stitches and a pattern that lends itself to a large bulky look. Bargello rugs, although very attractive, are not durable and should be used in little traveled areas or as wall hangings.

As of this writing, some acrylic tapestry yarns are being introduced in needlepoint shops. Some of them are very good but not yet available in the color selections we are accustomed to. I suggest that you test a small quantity and judge for yourself.

I would like to add that on a given needlework design, it is possible to use more than one type of yarn as long as it covers your canvas.

Estimating Yarns

THE ability to select and estimate the amount of yarn needed for a project plays a very important part in designing your own needlepoint. You cannot expect a shop owner to spend hours estimating yarns and color blends for your own design in return for the sale of a few ounces of yarn. Learn to do it yourself and then if you should run short, you will have no one but yourself to blame.

Yarns and threads are marketed in standard packages. Wool, cotton, rayon, and silk are available in small skeins of about eight or ten yards or meters. A meter is a European unit of linear measure and is equivalent to 1.093 yards. This means that a skein of ten meters will be slightly longer than ten yards and therefore it is safe to figure all your yarns and threads in yards and perhaps, at the end, you may have a few strands left over which is certainly a lot better than being short.

Some tapestry yarns are available in larger skeins with the proper yardage indicated on the package. Persian yarn is also sold by the pound. Paternayan persian yarn comes in four-ounce uncut skeins. When cut at both ends, they yield about 200 three-ply 32-inch strands of yarn. This is my favorite length because when the needle is threaded, there is a foldover of several inches and it's very comfortable to work with.

Test your projected pattern on a small piece of canvas. For a linear pattern work up a full line to see how many strands it takes. Count the number of lines that fit into one inch of your design then multiply the two numbers.

Therefore, if you use four strands of yarn to complete a given line of bargello, and it takes three lines to one inch of pattern, you will need thirty lines to finish a 10-inch pattern. Thirty lines times four strands will require 120 strands of yarn for your project. Divide by color, and add 10% to allow for errors. For a patterned bargello, work up one or two complete pattern units. Measure the unit in length and in width and figure out how many of these units will fit into the projected work. Count the strands you used in each color for each unit and do some simple multiplication to get the sum total. Don't forget to include the half patterns that border your design and add 10%.

At first you will make mistakes and chances are you will either run short or will have much leftover yarn. After a time, your eye will become trained and your estimates will become more accurate as a result.

About Canvas

ANVAS used for needlepoint is an open-mesh, even-weave cotton fabric. It is sized or starched for extra firmness that gives support and an even quality to the needlepoint stitches.

Single mesh or mono canvas has single threads running horizontally and vertically, forming even little squares as they cross each other.

Double mesh or duo canvas has double threads criss-crossing each other. The size of the little squares and their number to the inch represents the gauge or number of the canvas. Therefore if the canvas measures twelve squares to an inch, it is #12 canvas.

The single-mesh canvas is recommended for bargello stitchery in preference to the double mesh. This is because the long upright stitches will cover single-mesh canvas more readily.

Canvas is available in a large selection of mesh sizes. The gauge you choose has to be compatible with the yarn; that is, the yarn must cover the canvas without distorting the mesh.

Canvas comes in colors. The most popular are white and a light brown. Both are satisfactory and may be used for the same purpose. When working with white or very light yarns, white canvas may be more desirable; however, when working with very dark or black yarns the white canvas will show through and this is when a brown canvas is recommended.

Dark canvas is of firmer texture and will not show through white yarn, so that when it is necessary to use both light and dark yarns, it is best to choose the darker canvas.

If you are unable to find dark canvas, tint the white one. Use a strong infusion of tea (three tea bags steeped for ten minutes in a cup of boiling water and cooled) or standard household tint such as Rit or Tintex.

Place the cooled tea or tinting solution in a shallow pan or basin and dip the canvas into it very quickly. Pin the canvas to a blocking board and let dry at room temperature. It is not necessary to tint the canvas very dark, only just to shade over the stark whiteness.

Make certain that the tinting solution is cool. A hot solution will soften the sizing in your canvas.

When the tinted canvas is dry, trim the rough edges, tape, and proceed with your bargello design. Use paper or plastic tape for rough edges. Never use surgical or cellophane tape. The best way to edge canvas is with a close blanket stitch if your sewing machine is equipped with such an attachment. Bias tape stitched all around the edge is excellent, as is an edging of several rows of straight or zig-zag machine stitching.

If the canvas to be tinted is too large to handle, pin it to a board, pour the tinting solution in a bowl, and brush it on the canvas with a soft brush. Steam it lightly with a damp towel and hot iron to prevent it from puckering, and let dry. Tint canvas light beige or light gray. Don't use very dark or bright colors.

In selecting canvas, use the very best quality available. The difference in price per 18 by 18 square of canvas is negligible and it makes a world of difference in the finished article. A good quality canvas is firm but not rigid. The mesh is very even and the threads look very straight and true. Knots that re-tie thread breaks are few and barely visible.

About Needles: Tapestry needles have blunt points and a large eye. They should slide easily through the canvas mesh. Ask for them by number—the larger the number, the smaller the needle.

Mono canvas #12 will accommodate a #18 needle.

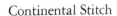

Continental Stitch

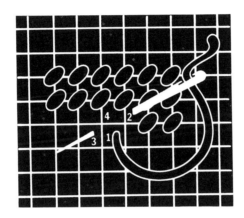

Basket-Weave Stitch

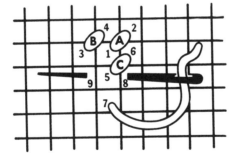

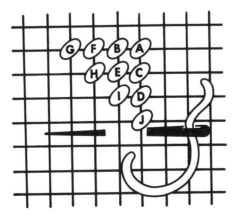

About Color

ONE of the most spectacular features about tapestry yarns is their enormous range of colors. Each color family is subdivided into four to sometimes eight graduated shades.

The art of blending color is a highly specialized one. It is a science in itself. A trained eye for color is not a matter of chance or a two-month job in a needlepoint shop. It is a combination of special talents plus many years of experience.

It is therefore impossible to teach professional expertise in a few short paragraphs. However, I would like to show you how to look at colors and how to be able to select those that are right for you.

To begin with, if you are really serious about working out your own designs and color blends you must start building a library of yarns. A color chart with little one-inch strips of yarn samples tacked to a cardboard is good only as a reference guide to available colors. It is not satisfactory when working out color blends.

For this you must have a handful or a small skein of yarn in as many colors as you can manage. At first buy only your favorite colors. Include all the shadings available in each of these colors. Keep these skeins loosely tied and tagged with the manufacturer's name and color number. Keep them hanging on a peg board or a revolving tie rack rather than in a box. Most tapestry yarns are available in small skeins that retail for about 25 cents. A fifty-color sampler will cost around $12.50. Add two or three squares of canvas for working up samples and a few needles and you are on your way.

Don't wait until you plan a needlepoint project. Begin to work with your color samples right away. Place a few of your favorite shades on a piece of white fabric. Move them around a bit. Replace some of the colors with a darker value within their own family. See how the rest of the colors are affected. Do you still like that green as much? How about the rust? Would it look better replaced with a lighter, brighter shade? Try it and see. Now take all the colors and place them on a black background. Keep changing the shades and see how the other colors are affected. Unlike oil paints, you cannot mix color pigments to achieve a desired shade. Wool yarns affect each other in certain ways and the result has a pleasant effect on you or not.

Watch what happens when you place a sky blue next to a bright red. The blue looks gray and the red seems too bright. Replace the blue with another one that has a purple tone and the effect is altogether different.

A medium lavender will make the red look softer and a bright green will make it vibrate. Several very bright colors on a white background will look unpleasant. The same colors on a black background will have a vibrant glow like stained glass. After a while you will begin to understand. Colors affect us like music. It isn't the single note but a combination of many notes played a certain way that spell a tune. From time to time enlarge your collection. Don't be afraid of using new colors. Sometimes a seemingly strange shade will have a wonderful effect in a most unexpected way.

When you are ready to design a new needlepoint project, select the colors you plan to use and place them on a piece of furniture in the room they are intended for. Leave them there for several days and examine them in daylight, twilight, and artificial light. Decide when you will use the room most often and gear the colors for that time of day and the available light. Keep moving the colors and replacing some with other shades. When it is right, you will know that very minute. If you keep selecting each needlepoint color blend in this manner, then no matter how different the designs will be, they will always "live" well together. They will reflect your personality, your taste, and your feeling about color.

Experiment with color another way. Work up small samples in two colors. Reverse the colors on another sample and see what happens. Do a patchwork design using the same pattern in every possible color combination or use a number of different patterns and textures all in the same color.

When you have a large background to do, combine two or three closely related shades instead of just one color. If you are working with three strands of persian yarn, buy three shades and use one strand from each. If you are working with only two strands, use two shades. The effect will be very beautiful. Be sure to select shades that are very close; otherwise the background will look "tweedy."

Throughout the book I have presented a large and varied collection of needlepoint designs based on the bargello stitch. Graph and yarn estimates are included whenever possible. I hope you enjoy using them. Some of the designs use the single cross stitch as a background. See page 25 for the ways of working this in either continental or basket weave.

Graph for Plate 2, page 34

Graph for Plate 3, page 35

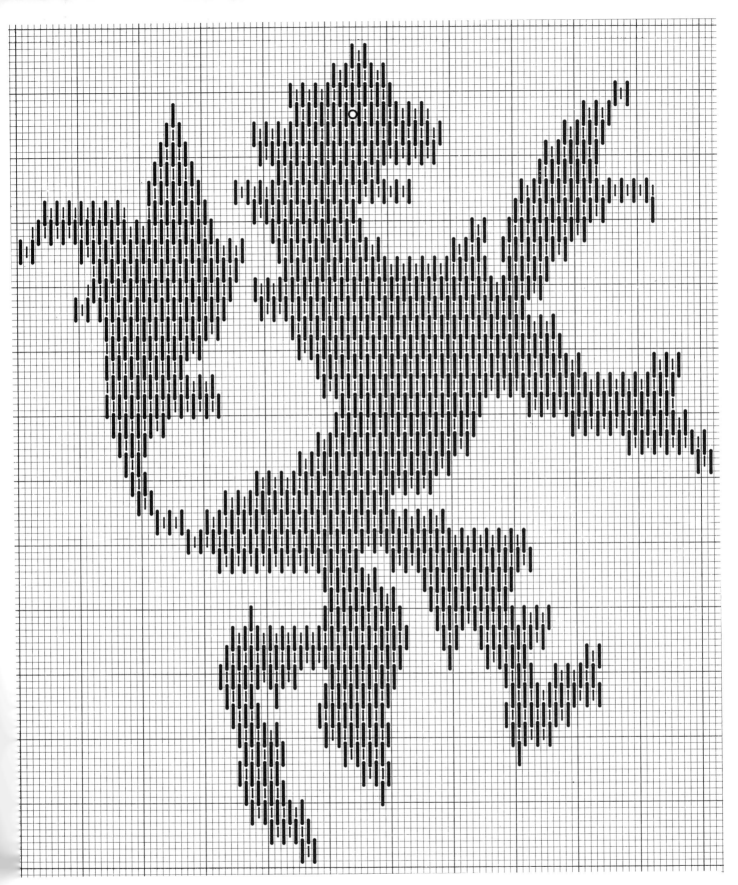

Graph for Plate 4, page 36

Plate 1. Peacock. A very elegant design worked on a painted canvas with rayon threads and small beads. The background is worked with six-strand embroidery floss. The head and background are worked in continental stitch and the rest of the peacock is worked in long and short bargello stitches better known as parisian stitches. The beads are placed at certain intervals instead of the short stitches.

Materials needed for this design are one square of #14 canvas 20 by 20. (Allow a two-inch margin all around.) Two skeins each of rayon thread in dark green, light green, lavender, lavender rose, purple, turquoise, and light turquoise, ten skeins of white cotton embroidery thread for background, and two small skeins gold. Small bright-colored glass beads, one package each of green, purple, pink, and turquoise. Tapestry needle and beading needle.

This design may be worked with all-cotton threads or with two strands of persian yarn with excellent results. Rayon and cotton threads must be doubled for bargello and used singly for continental stitches. To work continental stitch, see right. *Based on a drawing by Patricia Weiss.*

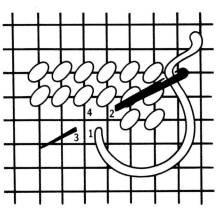

Plate 2. Patchwork design worked on 18 by 20 #12 canvas with three-ply persian yarn. Three small skeins in dark red and orange and two skeins in all other colors. Colors may be changed if desired. For graph see page 29

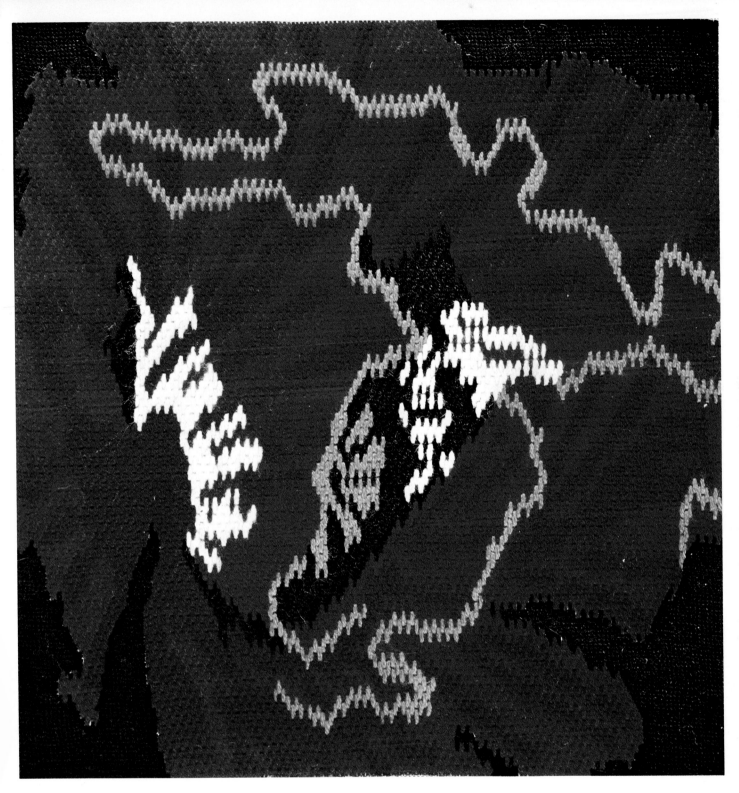

Plate 3. Magnificent red poppy worked on a painted canvas 18 by 18. Follow graph outline and work in brick stitch. Materials needed are two ounces persian yarn bright red, one ounce black, one ounce dark red, two small skeins each in white and bright orange. Backround may be worked in continental or brick stitch. *Based on a drawing, courtesy Suzy Girard, Inc., New York City.* For graph see page 30.

Plate 4. Coat of arms on 18 by 20 #12 canvas with three-ply persian yarn and metallic gold color thread. The entire design is worked in parisian stitch. The longer stitches are worked first in red and the smaller stitches placed afterward in gold. Entire background worked in parisian stitch in royal blue. Border in gold. Materials needed are four ounces royal blue, two ounces red, and three small skeins metallic gold. For graph see page 31

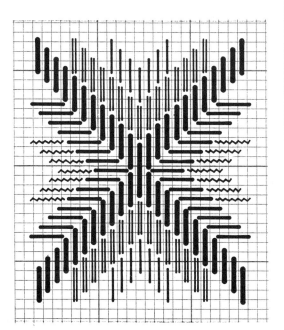

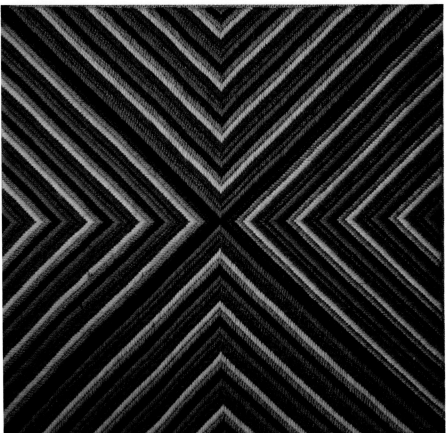

Plate 5. Angled bargello design has many possibilities. The center line is not really an X but rather two Vs point to point. These are the lead lines. Continue by working each angle separately. The color sequence may be the same in all four areas or it may be used in reverse as in this design. Change colors or use two colors only. Stripes may be wider or in random widths. Each section may be worked in a different color.

Plate 6. Another angled design. Looks best as a diamond-shaped pillow or picture. Both designs require four ounces of assorted-color persian yarn for a #12 or #14 canvas. 16 by 16.

Plates 7 and 8.   Two bargello designs with an open background. An even-weave white canvas has a quality all its own and may become an integral part of a design.

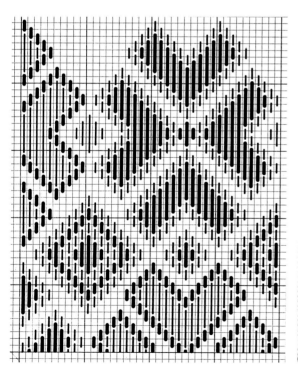

Plate 9. Bargello in the round. May be displayed horizontally or vertically. An excellent design for upholstering small footstools. Center may be used for a favorite design done in continental stitch. An 18 by 20 canvas requires six ounces of persian yarn in assorted colors. Stitches may be worked over four or six strands of canvas.

Plate 10. A very popular three-dimensional design worked in ten colors. The interesting effect is achieved through the proper shading. There are five shades of one family of color plus a black for the main pattern. The centers are worked with three shades of gray plus white. Colors may be changed but the gradation of shades must be the same. A #12 canvas 20 by 20 requires about one ounce persian yarn in each color. *Worked by Rita Scheuer.*

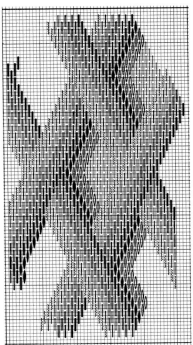

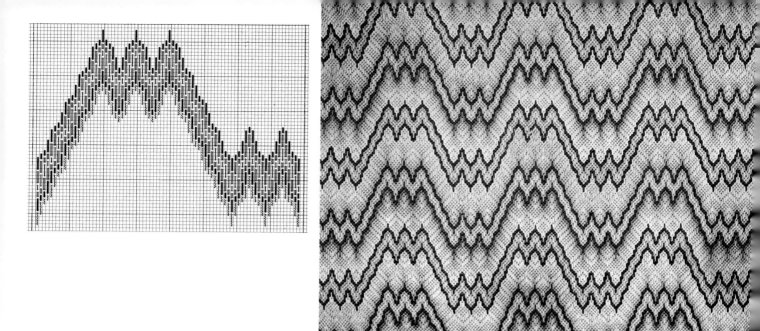

Plate 11. An antique bargello design worked with long and short stitches. Embroidery cotton on linen.

Plate 12. Fish. Modern design with continental stitch and long bargello stitches in random stripes. *Based on a drawing, "Fish Eaters," courtesy denà designs.*

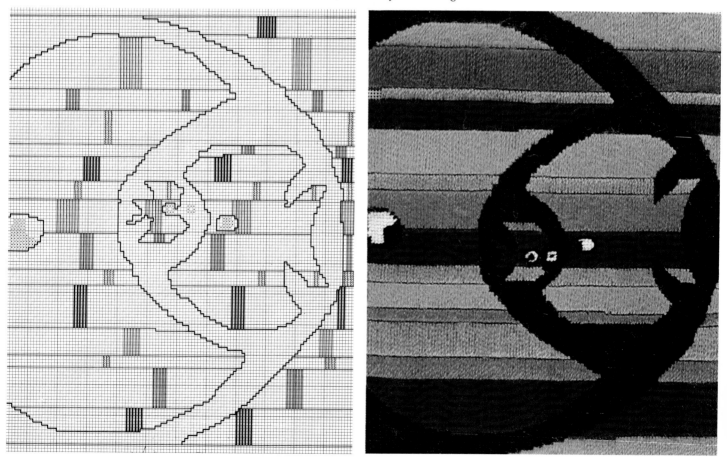

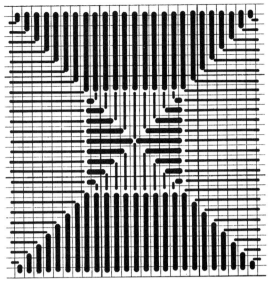

Plate 13. Bold squares with mitered bargello. Each square requires two strands of persian yarn in color and one-half strand in black. Very good for using up leftover yarns and for wall hangings with heavy rug yarn on #4 canvas.

Plate 14. Wedgwood. A very delicate design that looks lovely inside an antique frame. The bow pattern is worked in long random stitches (see graph) with six-strand embroidery cotton. The background is finished in continental stitch or basket weave (page 25). After the finished piece is blocked and just before it is framed, the white stitches are worked in a second layer in cotton or silk. This gives the design the raised look. You need four skeins of white cotton embroidery thread or two cotton and two silk. For the background, six skeins of blue cotton.

Plates 15 and 16. Two more carnation designs. The first is copied from an antique chair seat cover. It is fine for a large area because the design repeat is so wide. It may be made smaller by using only the carnations on a simple background. The second is a bolder more modern adaptation of the carnation. Each flower has the same outline but the color combination is different and the possibilities are limitless.

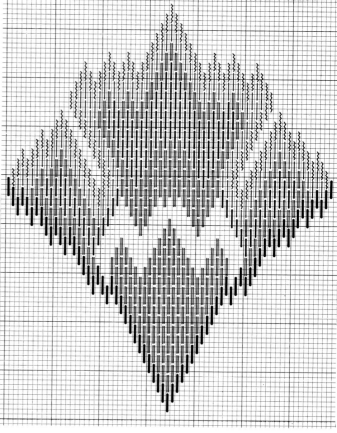

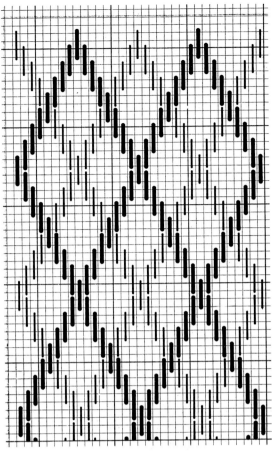

Plate 17. A small repeat design that may be used in many color combinations. Because of the small even-stitch pattern, it is an excellent choice for upholstery as well as small-area rugs.

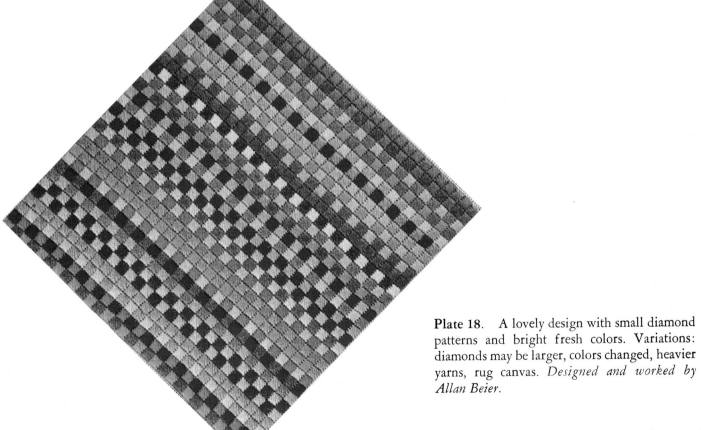

Plate 18. A lovely design with small diamond patterns and bright fresh colors. Variations: diamonds may be larger, colors changed, heavier yarns, rug canvas. *Designed and worked by Allan Beier.*

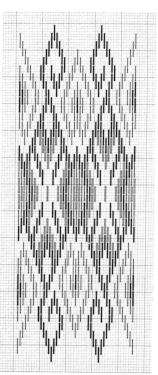

Plates 19 and 20. Two identical designs. One is worked in single stitches over six strands of canvas. The other one is worked in double stitches over four strands of canvas. Each is very handsome when worked in heavy rug yarn on #4 canvas.

Plate 21. Venice. Bargello and continental stitches on 22 by 18 #14 canvas. Two-ply persian yarn. One or two small skeins in each color indicated. Four skeins for sky. Mix one strand each of pale gray and pale blue gray. Like all patchwork designs, it is an excellent way to use up leftover yarns. *Based on a drawing, "Street Scene," courtesy denà designs.* For graph see page 50

Plate 22. Carnations. A very old and still popular design. One small skein of persian yarn in each color indicated will be sufficient for two flowers. Two ounces of yarn for background for 16 by 16 canvas. *Worked by Mrs. Florence Morris.*

Plate 23. Bargello blanket. Worked with leftover yarns as a sampler. Approximately sixty strands used in each square. Squares are worked individually on 8 by 8 #12 canvas. Allow one inch margin all around, leaving a finished area of 6 by 6. When all the twenty-five squares are finished, make sure they are perfectly square (pin to a board and steam if necessary). Trim all margins to ¼-inch all around. Overlap the margins and pin into place. Lift the blanket and hang on a wall. Adjust pins until it hangs right. Place on flat surface and baste the overlapped margins. Remove pins and machine stitch with two rows of plain or zig-zag stitches all around. Place criss-cross of ¼-inch black ribbon to cover the white margins. Tack ribbons securely with small stitches. Line the blanket with a soft fabric. Blanket may be made larger or smaller.

For graphs see page 51

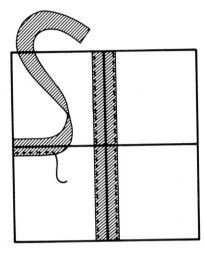

Plate 24. Tiger. A random width bargello on a painted canvas. Has a textured effect. Materials needed are two ounces each black and gold persian yarn on 14 by 16 #12 canvas. *Based on a drawing, courtesy Suzy Girard, Inc.*

Optical illusions. Work in three colors. The blocks may be worked shorter or longer. Looks well as a pillow, wall hanging or small area rug in bulky yarn.

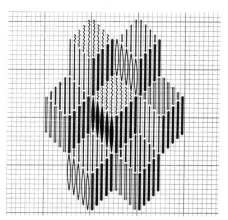

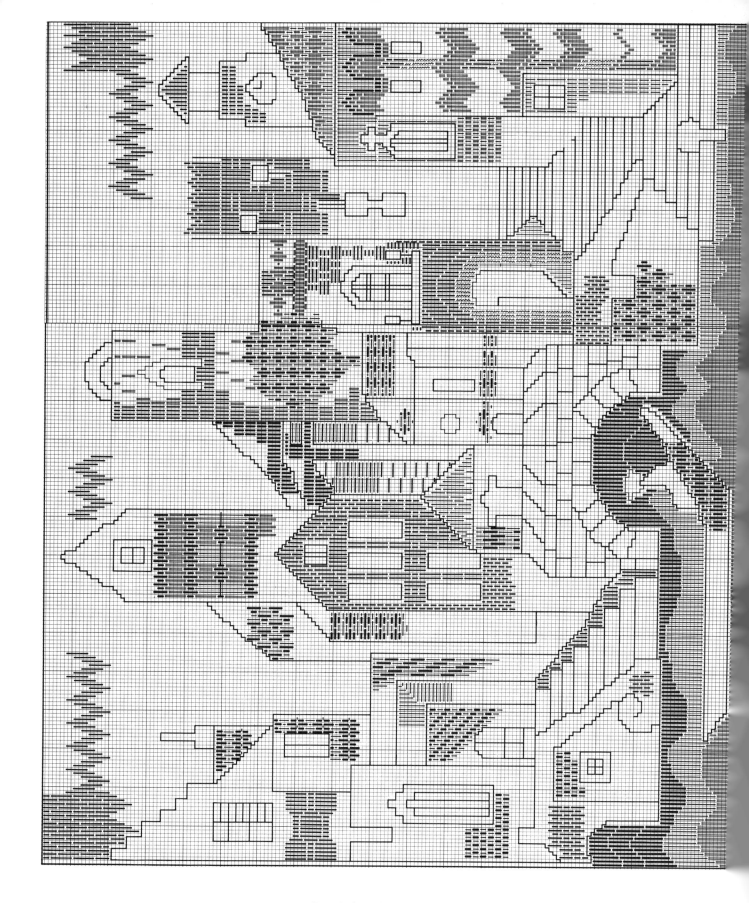

Graph for Plate 21, page 45

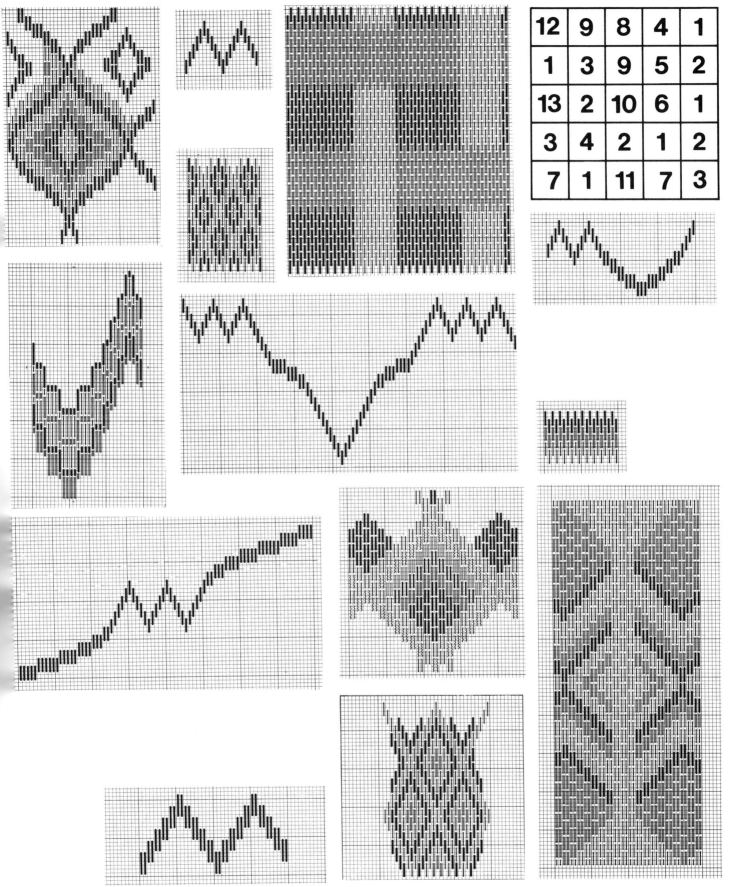

12	9	8	4	1
1	3	9	5	2
13	2	10	6	1
3	4	2	1	2
7	1	11	7	3

Graphs for Plate 23, page 47

Bargello as Fabric

BARGELLO needlework on canvas produces an excellent fabric that is suitable for handbags, belts, mittens, as well as various articles of clothing. This is primarily a winter-weight fabric, and if you bear this in mind you can make a variety of attractive things that are soft and warm and wear for a long time.

If you are interested in making some articles of clothing with bargello fabric, I suggest that you read this chapter very carefully.

First, you must understand your materials and what they can do for you. Canvas that is used for needlework is an even-weave cotton mesh that has been sized or starched to give it firmness. This firmness is important only during the time the stitches are being worked. The constant handling of the work and the weight of the yarn tend to soften the canvas somewhat, but not enough to make it suitable for clothing. In addition to this, the yarn makes the fabric heavy and a small tunic may end up weighing a pound or more. To solve this problem, you must use less yarn. And so, working the same pattern and gauge of canvas, use a thinner yarn. A #12 mono canvas that normally takes three-ply persian yarn should be worked with only two-ply. The canvas will show through, of course, and you solve that by dipping the finished article in hot water. This accomplishes a dual purpose: washing away the sizing and shrinking your canvas just enough to bring it tighter around your stitches. Result: a soft and light woolen fabric. A few drops of Woolite added to the water will help make the wool softer but is not absolutely essential.

The hot-water dipping should be done quickly. Don't soak the article in water for longer than a minute. Roll it in a thick terry cloth towel and unroll it immediately. Let it finish drying at room temperature.

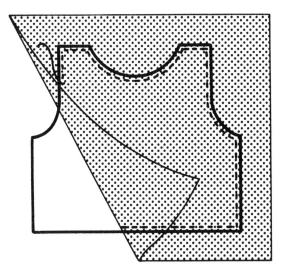

To make a tunic or vest, select a pattern from a standard pattern book. For a first project, make it simple: no buttons, no pockets, and a minimum number of darts. Use #12 mono canvas and two-ply strands of a three-ply persian wool yarn. The pattern should be one size larger than you normally take. Place paper pattern *under* the canvas. (If pattern needs adjusting it must be done first.) Line up the strands of the canvas with the arrows on the pattern that indicate the straight of the fabric. Pin canvas to the paper pattern. Notice that the pattern has two outlines. One is the cutting outline, thick and heavy. The other is a little finer and roughly one inch inside the cutting line. This indicates the sewing line. See diagram.

Outline any darts and notches inside the pattern with one strand of yarn slightly darker than the canvas. This is so it will be visible during the time it is being embroidered. But in case some of the bargello stitches cover it, it would become invisible and could be left alone. (This is a good way to mark any needlepoint canvas.)

Cut out the pattern 1/4 inch outside the cutting outline. Unpin the pattern and very gently tear away the paper from the canvas along the darts and notches so as not to disturb the outline stitches. There is no need to outline the sewing line. Simply measure the distance between the cutting and the sewing outlines and stay within this margin as you work your bargello pattern. One or two stitches over the line hardly matter, but keep most of the margin clear or there will be a bulky seam. Do not tape edges. Protect the cut edge with two or three rows of open zig-zag machine stitching, or in the absence of a zig-zag attachment work several rows of large machine stitches all around the cut pattern outline. Keep the rows of stitches slightly apart.

This is very important because when you dip the finished

canvas in hot water the rough edges will unravel immediately if not properly finished. Tape will soften in hot water and will fall apart.

Once the canvas pattern is prepared, work the pattern with two strands of persian yarn. Keep the wrong side of the canvas free of knots and tail ends. When all the pieces of the pattern are finished, dip them in a basin of hot water for about a minute. Roll quickly in a thick towel. Unroll immediately, shape with your fingers, or, if the pieces of fabric are large, pin them to a board with aluminum push pins or nails. Do not stretch too much. Let dry at room temperature. If not soft enough, repeat "washing process."

Handle the finished bargello like any other fabric. Sew and line according to pattern instructions. This washing and shrinking method may be used whenever bargello stitches seem too tight and the canvas shows through.

At this point I would like to add some helpful hints:

Use persian yarn only. The finishing method described above does not work out too well with cotton or acrylic fibers. Test your materials before anticipating a large project. Work up a test piece of canvas first, using the same yarn and pattern that will be used on the project. Wash and dry the sample according to directions, and check the results carefully. With the increased popularity in needlepoint media, there is a larger number of canvas distributors. Although most canvas is adequate for standard bargello, not all of it is recommended for clothing. Sometimes a canvas is too soft to hold its shape during stitching and sometimes the sizing used is of a permanent nature and will not wash away. Shop around to find the best.

Choose a pattern that is not involved and would not require too much cutting and rethreading of yarns. Keep stitches soft, and a maximum length of six strands of canvas. Remember to line up the pattern at seams so that when the garment is sewn together it looks professional. Bear in mind also that canvas is not perfectly square. Although it can be worked in the length or the width with excellent results, the pattern will be slightly different. You might not be able to notice it on two different pillows, but it will most certainly make a difference if you work, say, the back of a tunic in the width and the front in the length of your canvas. The seams will not line up and no amount of pulling or stretching will help.

May I also remind you that this is not a lesson in sewing but only in preparing a bargello canvas for use as fabric. If you are not very adept at dressmaking, do have your tunic finished professionally.

Bargello stitchery may be used as decorative embroidery on any even-weave fabric. Use either linear patterns leaving several strands of fabric in between lines or use patterns illustrated here and on page 56 (1B). Bargello borders worked with cotton embroidery floss look lovely on place mats or small tablecloths. Remember to use an even-weave single-mesh fabric.

Bargello stitchery should not be machine washed because the long stitches tend to twist. Hand wash or dry clean only, and don't use any marking pens at any time.

Instructions for making Christmas Boot illustrated below: Place design on an 18x18 square #12 canvas. Begin at center and work up half a lead line to the right. Begin at center and finish lead line to the left. Following the general outline of boot as shown, work bargello over six strands of canvas. Color sequence is one line red, two green, one white, one green, and repeat. When the entire boot is finished, trace the outline and transfer it to a piece of velvet or similar soft fabric in red or green. Machine stitch on three sides right sides together leaving bottom open. Trim edges to ¼ inch and turn over. Fold boot so that the sides line up and pin at several points to keep in place. To make the sole, measure the distance between tip of boot and center fold and trace this line on paper. Draw an oval shape to incorporate this line not more than 3½ inches at the widest point. Allow one inch for margin. Cut two. Sew together right sides in. Turn out and pin the sole to the bottom of boot. Since it is not a shoe it does not have to be a perfect sole. It is made only to keep the boot from falling over. Slip stitch with matching yarn all around the bottom and instep of boot. Leave top open. It will stand if filled with toys, candy canes, or greens. Add a bow if you wish.

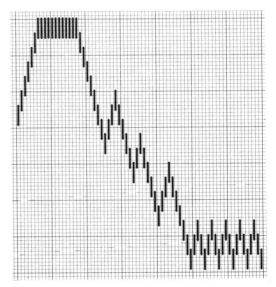

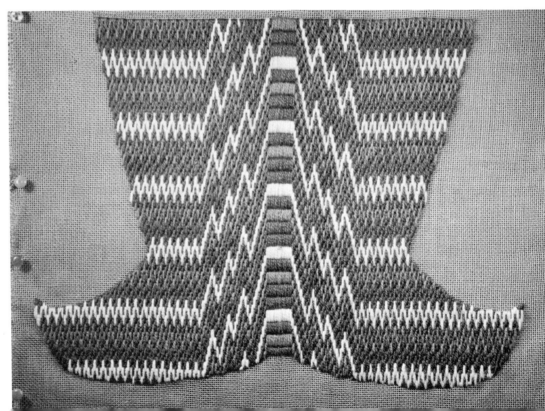

When it is necessary to rip out any portion of a bargello design there is a right way to do this. Unless it is absolutely necessary to save the bit of yarn, don't pick out the thread stitch by stitch. This is time consuming and it frays the yarn. Decide what area must be cut away, slip a sharp pointed embroidery scissors under the line of bargello on the right side of the work, and cut through the center of the stitches (B). Turn canvas over on the wrong side, pull out cut thread, undo several stitches on each end of the cut-out area, enough to thread the needle at each end, and tuck in the ends (C). Now turn work right side up (D) and fill in the open area with proper stitches.

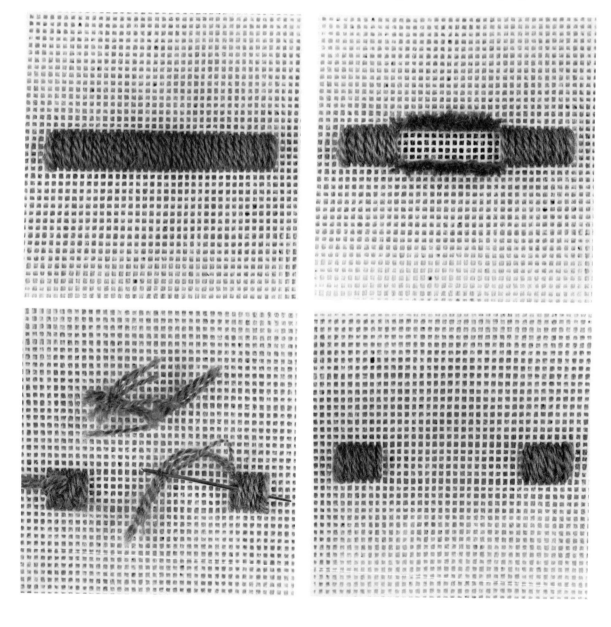

Mitering

ITERING is easy and fun to do. Begin by working up a line of bargello with very long stitches. After working about three or four inches, begin mitering by making the stitches shorter on one side. Make them shorter by one strand of canvas only. The diminishing stitches should be at the top of your line while the bottom line remains the same. When the stitch is only over one strand of canvas, take the next stitch at right angles to the little one. Work this line in reverse beginning with the very smallest and ending with the largest stitch. Keep the outside line straight and increase the inner line so that each stitch meets its counterpart in the same square of canvas. When the largest stitches meet, continue working a line of straight stitches for as long as you want the frame to be. Repeat mitering process in all four corners. Make sure all opposite sides are equal. Count the stitches to be sure.

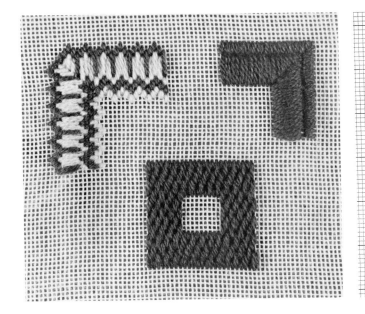

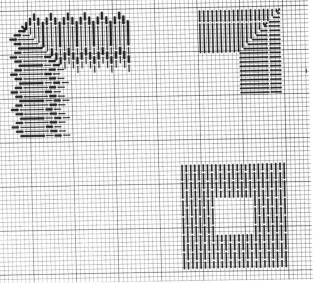

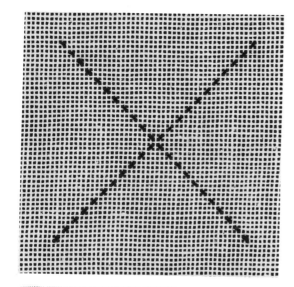

Any linear design may be mitered to form a corner. The longer the stitch the deeper the miter. Two or more mitered frames in various widths are very attractive when worked around standard needlepoint. Borders such as those on page 55 may be mitered singly or in sets to be used on picture frames or table linens. If the border is very decorative, there is no need to fill in the background. Canvas or linen or any even-weave fabric are very pleasing to the eye and make a lovely background for bargello.

Study the designs on pages 60, 61, 63, 67, 69 (lower left), 70, 71 (bottom), 76 (frames), 78. They are worked with four parts of the same design that have been mitered. The effect is often that of a kaleidoscope. In order to miter a more complicated design, criss-cross your canvas with two rows of fine stitches that form an X (top left) on your canvas and divide it in four equal parts. It is very important to take small even stitches in each canvas square as you work the lines. Use a thin thread in a shade slightly darker than your canvas. You will be able to see it while working on the design, but once covered it will not be necessary to take it out. The criss-cross line should be knotted and fastened to prevent it from shifting, but if you place the knots and the tacks on the outside of the line of your work, you can clip these when you are finished.

Work up one quarter of the design at a time. Shorten the last stitch of each line as it is placed into the criss-cross outline. See center left. Work each quarter of the design separately. To achieve a proper mitered look, all the corresponding stitches must fall into the same square of canvas. Try the simpler patterns first such as bottom right. This one is worked as a diamond and may be used as a repeat pattern.

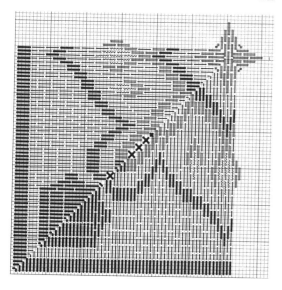

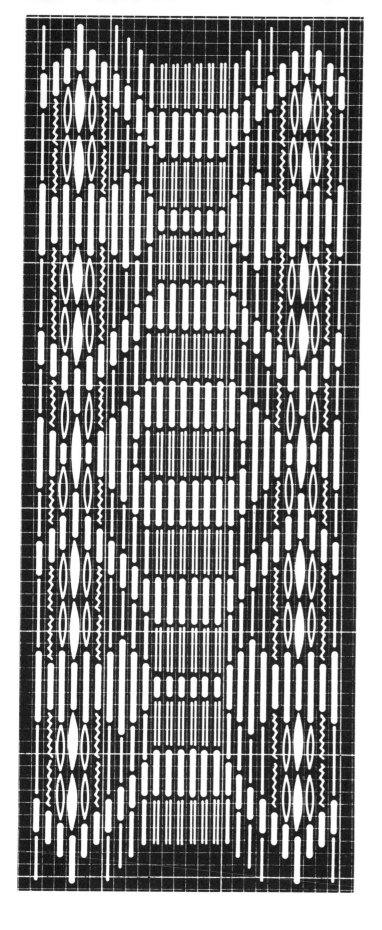

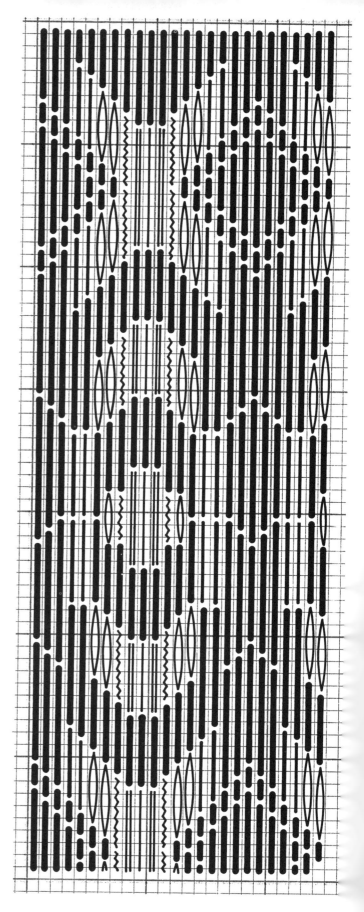

Graphs for Plates 26 and 26A, page 66

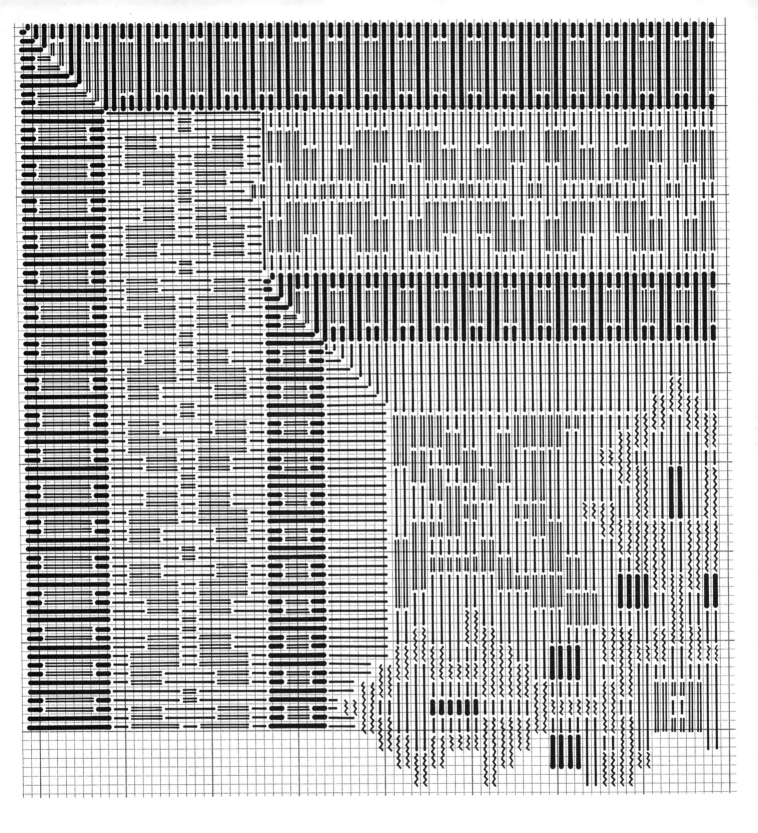

Graph for Plate 27, page 67

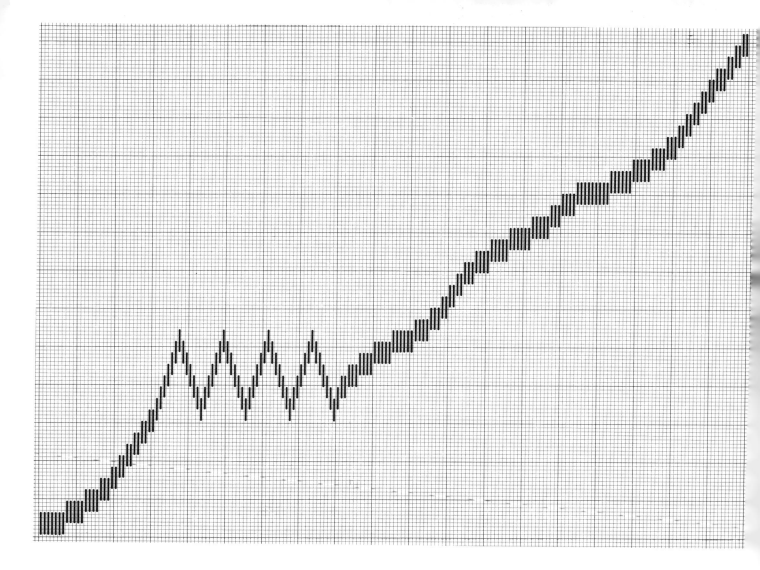

Graph for Plate 28, page 68

Plate 25. A lovely repeat pattern. Three-ply persian yarn on 12 by 12 #12 canvas. One small skein each yellow, light pink, and dark pink, two skeins each white and light green, and four skeins dark green. Opposite and below, left. *Designed and worked by Elise Silverstein.*

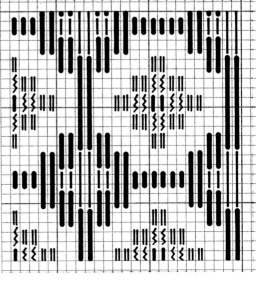

Plate 26. A different way to work two bargello designs. Work all the colors vertically beginning at the top right. Work each color downward, leaving the black area to be filled in later. Bring all the threads of one color down, and after completing the first half of the design work the threads in reverse upward to complete the second half of the design (see page 62, right). When all the colors are completed, fill in the black background in the conventional manner working right to left or left to right. This is a very good design for rugs. For graphs see page 62

Plate 27. Framed bargello design. Some borders are mitered and others are not. Borders may be repeated to enlarge design or may be used to frame other bargello designs. This 16 by 16 square #12 canvas requires 1½ ounces each blue, green, and red persian yarn and two small skeins bright gold. *Designed and worked by Elise Silverstein.* For graph see page 63

Opposite, for graph see page 64

Plate 28. Orange flame design (opposite). A simple linear pattern that achieves importance by the use of color and shading. Place your lead line and follow it one line at a time. There are three shades of wine red, five shades of hot orange, and one bright lemon yellow. Reverse colors in a mirror image. Repeat design as often as necessary. A #12 canvas 18 by 20 design requires two small skeins of darkest wine and lemon yellow and four small skeins in each of the other color. Stitches are worked over six strands of canvas. *Designed and worked by Elise Silverstein.*

Plate 29. The India influence. Turquoise, red, and gold. This is mitered bargello and you can see the small stitches that indicate the division of the four quarters. At this point the black outline may continue as the background. Keep working it out and mitering at the corner until the design is squared off.

Plate 30. A very attractive design with a large repeat. It is very easy to work out and looks best in black and white plus one. That is, you may change the red but keep the white and black as shown.

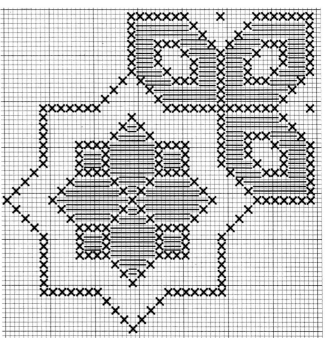

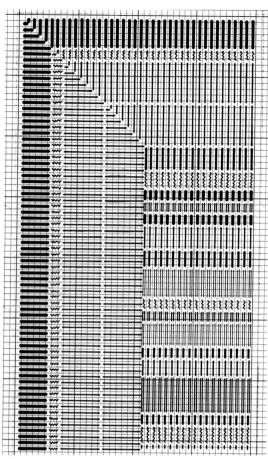

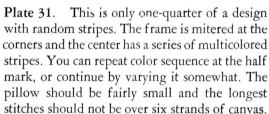

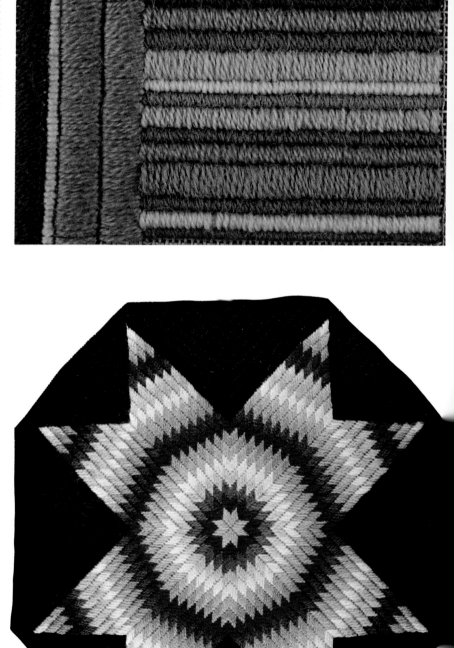

Plate 31. This is only one-quarter of a design with random stripes. The frame is mitered at the corners and the center has a series of multicolored stripes. You can repeat color sequence at the half mark, or continue by varying it somewhat. The pillow should be fairly small and the longest stitches should not be over six strands of canvas.

Plate 32. Patchwork design. Star begins with a mitered bargello center but afterward it is worked in the round. Each "patch" is four stitches and you work each in a circle changing direction as you cross the miter line. Study the design and graph on the facing page carefully, and after a little practice you will find it quite easy.

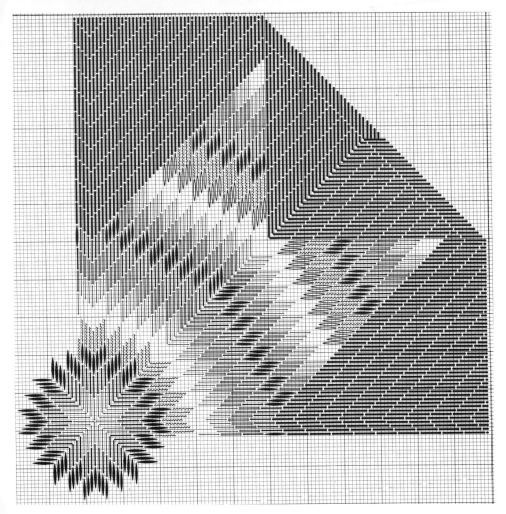

Plate 34. An interesting modern design in blue, brown, and pearls. Again we have the parisian stitch with some of the short stitches left out and replaced with small pearls. This idea may be used for larger wall hangings using heavy rug yarns and large ceramic beads.

Plate 33. Another star design in a different color combination. The background may be finished in a square or octagon shape.

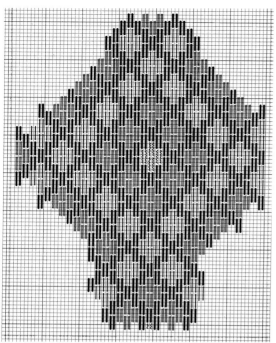

Plates 35 and 36. Tiny squares are very versatile. The dark brown outlines form a graph-like pattern that may be used in countless ways. Here we have small rust-colored diamonds inside larger blue diamonds. The outlines may be larger and the colors may vary. It looks beautiful in only two colors and very striking with a confetti spray of multicolor yarns.

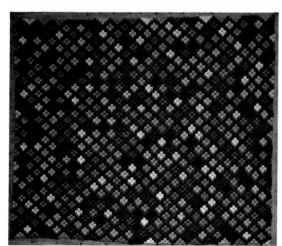

Plate 37. The rose design is taken from a cross stitch pattern. Each stitch is over four strands of canvas and every four bargello stitches represent one cross stitch. Because of the nature of the stitches, the bargello looks distorted and the canvas is pulled where the stitches meet. Dip the finished canvas in hot water to shrink the canvas and fluff out the yarn.

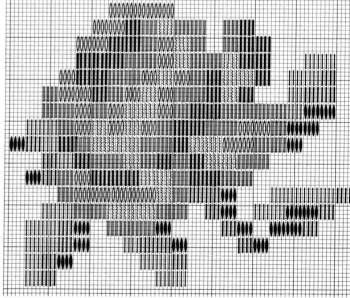

Plate 38. A patchwork design selection in a white frame. No need to use all the patterns. Use only two or three and alternate them or use only one in different color combinations. By adding an extra line of white inside each diamond pattern, the centers become smaller and may be filled with clear bright colors in plain stitches.

Plates 39 to 43. Five antique Turkish designs that resemble bargello. On page 17 several base patterns are worked out to help you with these designs. They are most attractive and may be used as pillows or as rugs. *Courtesy Persian Gallery, Inc., New York City.*

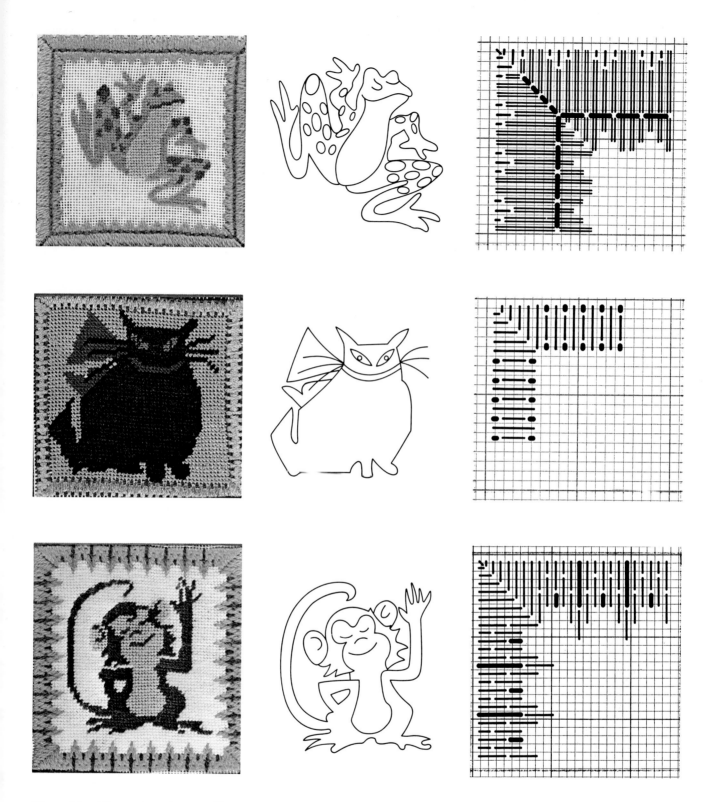

Plate 44. Three charming needle-point designs for continental stitch with bargello borders that enlarge a tiny pillow. *Based on drawings, courtesy Suzy Girard, Inc.*

Plate 45.   American wing chair, *c.*1725. The Metropolitan Museum of Art, Gift of Mrs. J. Insley Blair, 1950.

For graph see page 8

Plate 46. Turquoise stars on white background. An interesting mitered bargello repeat pattern. May be worked in one or more colors. A #12 canvas 16 by 16 requires two ounces each turquoise and white persian yarn. For graph see page 82

Plate 47. Examples of bargello as fabric: dog coat; belt; handbag; mittens; Christmas boot. See page 57.

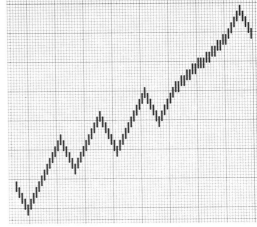

Plate 48. Three Wise Men. A handsome design with various bargello stitches. The faces and hands are worked in encroaching gobelin. All the stitches are indicated in the graph. This design is very striking on a larger mesh canvas with heavy rug yarns to be used as wall hanging. *Designed and worked by denà designs, Inc.*

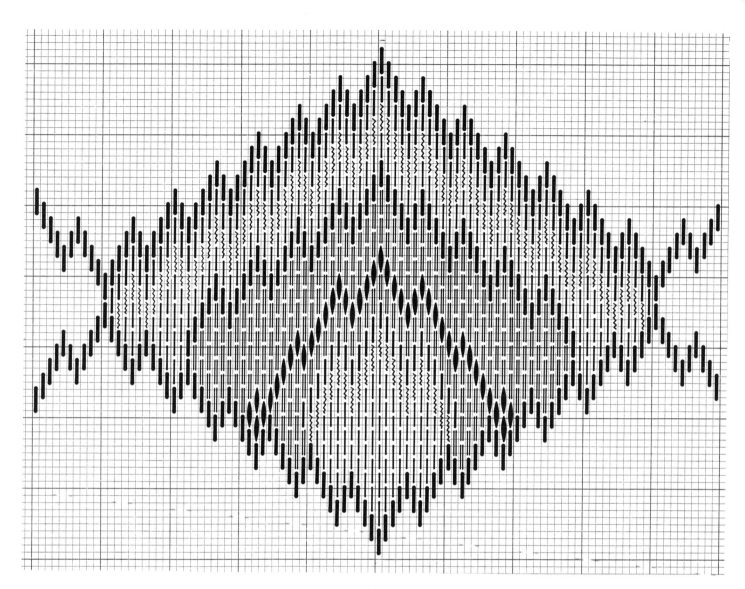

Graph for Plate 45, page 77

Graph for Plate 46, page 78

"Patterns"

Small open patterns are very useful and very versatile. They may be made smaller and filled with a variety of colors like bright flowers. They may be larger and used as patchwork outlines, or one may be opened large enough to accommodate a small picture worked in continental stitch (page 25) and then the background finished in bargello.

Some interesting patterns with long bargello stitches to be used as small pictures or in heavy yarn as small area rugs are shown on pages 83-86. Work these various small repeat patterns in black and white or any two-color combination.

Optical illusions. Work in three colors. The blocks may be worked shorter or longer. Looks well as a pillow, wall hanging or small area rug in bulky yarn.

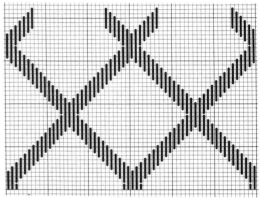

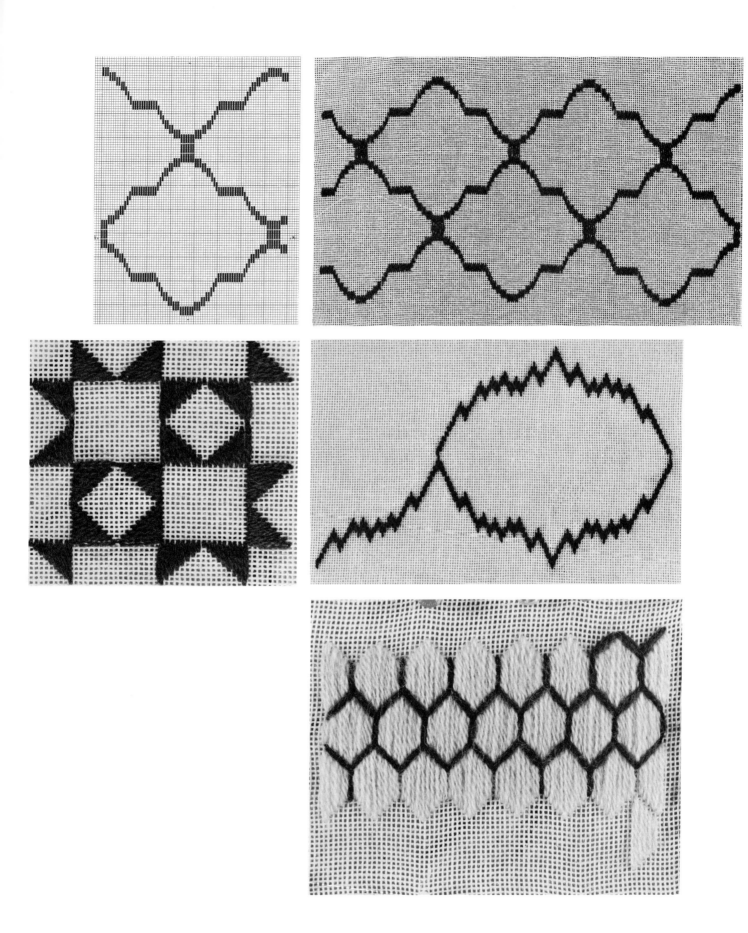

Optical illusions. Work in three colors. The blocks may be worked shorter or longer. Looks well as a pillow, wall hanging or small area rug in bulky yarn.

Free-Form Bargello

A new and interesting approach to bargello design is the free-form outline. Use the parisian or brick stitch, and following outlines at right practice the vertical, horizontal, and diagonal lines first. Study the stitches and then try your hand at a free-form line—first with the brick stitch and then with the parisian. The brick stitches are all the same size and fit together in an interlocking fashion. In the first line the stitches are worked in the stagger system (you work a stitch and skip one). The next row fills in the skipped stitches at the half mark. To work a free-form outline combine the horizontal, vertical, and diagonal lines to form a snaky line. Practice this and study photographs at right. The last is an open pattern outline very much like the one used in the carnation on the next page. You can see how free-form outlines can open unlimited possibilities in bargello design.

Brick Stitch

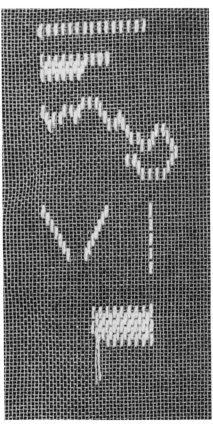

Parisian Stitch

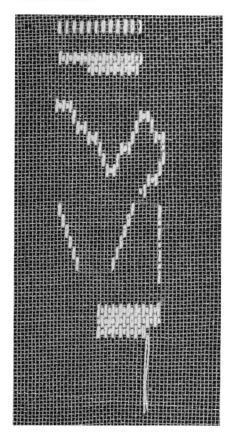

An extra stitch or two in either direction will alter the outline. Since all the stitches are of equal size and single steps, it is a very simple matter to design a small pattern that would fit inside the outline. The carnations (page 42) are one such example. The outlines may also be filled in with continental stitches using a painted design or one taken from a graph.

The parisian stitch is achieved by alternating large and small stitches. The large stitches are generally worked over four strands of canvas and the small ones fit in between and are worked over the center two strands. Free-form outlines worked in parisian stitch are slightly different from the brick stitch. The diagonal lines are a little steeper and the small stitches will often give a finer detail to an outline. The small stitches may be replaced with small beads for added interest. A fine example is the peacock (page 33) or the small modern design (page 71, top right). Another way to use the parisian stitch is to replace the small stitches with a gold or silver metallic thread as in the coat of arms (page 36).

The coat of arms was worked over a painted design and this brings us to still another kind of free-form bargello. That is working upright stitches over a canvas that has been painted for a conventional continental needlepoint design.

The peacock (33), coat of arms (36), poppy (35), three wise men (80), and Venice (45), are all worked in free-form bargello on painted canvas. The peacock is worked in parisian interspersed with beads and some continental stitches. The coat of arms is also parisian but with golden threads instead of beads. The three wise men has many different bargello stitches plus an interesting kind of encroaching gobelin on the face and hands of the figures. (See diagram page 81). The fish (40) is worked in both continental and long upright stitches. Venice is like a patchwork design, each building in a different pattern. The tiger (48) is a random stitch. Random stitches are fun to do and produce some of the most interesting bargello designs. (See instructions on page 14).

A very attractive design worked in random stitch is the "white bows on blue" that looks more difficult than it actually is. See instructions on page 80.

To insert beads between bargello stitches, complete your

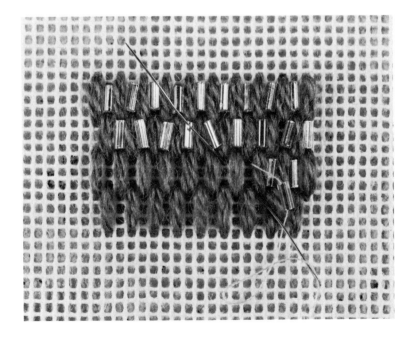

design leaving as many open spaces as you wish to replace with beads. This works best with the parisian stitch. Leave the small stitches out and make sure to work the other stitches in proper sequence. If the design is large and you are not certain as to the amount of beads you want to place, skip all the small stitches over the entire area. Add the beads as you see fit, then fill in the remaining open spots with yarn in the appropriate colors.

Beads are sewn on with a beading needle and a fine nylon thread. Some bead holes are so fine that the beading needle is almost impossible to thread. Check the beads and the appropriate needles before buying. Choose pretty glass beads and use matching thread to sew them on. Knot the thread and fasten firmly on the wrong side of work. Bring needle out in the same spot as would the yarn if you were doing a proper stitch. Thread your bead and then complete the stitch. Leave enough thread at the end to fasten securely. See page 89.